SPARK YOUR INNER TRUTH
- A Guided Journal -

Vanessa Sieger

Copyright © 2021, Vanessa Sieger-Wilson. All rights reserved.

How to use:

You can complete one page a day or the whole journal in a week, you are the soul pilot. Complete whatever questions you feel called to do and skip the ones that you do not. You can write, draw, or scribble your answers. If you feel your answers are more of the personal nature, you can scratch them out or draw on top of them to hide them.

When completing this journal to your satisfaction, a beautiful way to release your answers into the universe is to have a ceremonial burning of closure. You can burn this journal as a whole, or page by page. It is created with lightweight paper easy for safe burning, but please take all necessary precautions. When you choose to release your journal in closure, say "thank you" and share anything you wish as you let it go. Sit with how you feel and set your intentions.

You can choose to share your answers with others, or keep them completely confidential. Choose whatever process that helps you navigate through these questions.

If at any point you need more room to finish one of your answers, there are blank pages at the end of the book to continue your thoughts.

What intentions would I like to set in how I answer the questions within this journal?

How do I define happiness?

When do I feel most at peace?

If I could map out a perfect day, what would it look like?

What area of my life needs a little more attention?

Do I have resources, tools, and support? If so, what are they? If not, where do I find some?

Who/what am I thankful for that came into my life, but did not stay? Why?

What would help me trust the flow of life more?

What does love mean to me?

What are some events that shaped how I treat my relationships? The negative and the positive. Am I guarded or open? What can I do to ensure I am giving my best to the relationships in my life?

What has been my most painful heartache? Dig deep to find the lesson, what positive (even the smallest bit) came from this experience?

When have I felt the most passionate and alive? What is it about that time that impacted me so strongly?

If I had 5 minutes for the whole word to stop and listen to what I had to say, I would say….

What is one thing I would change in the world if I had the power to?

In what way am I influencing the world? In what way is the world influencing me?

How do I know if I am being true to my own values or falling off course?

Am I living a meaningful life? If my answer is no, what can I do to bring more meaning to my life?

Where can I be more gentle in my life? Is it towards a person, situation, or myself? How and why?

What advice would I pass on to the next generation that follows in my steps?

Do I feel that I have a past life/generational pattern or karma that I need to conquer? If so, what is it and how do I finally break the cycle?

Do any of the things that bothered me a few years ago matter to me today? What's changed?

What are my weaknesses?

What fills my energy up with positive feelings?

What have I done lately that I have not bragged about?

Clap Clap Clap – You Go!

If I could help one person see the true beauty inside themselves, who would it be and what would I show them?

Who are the top 5 people I surround myself with? Are they holding me back or feeding my soul?

1.

2.

3.

4.

5.

What in life, is beautiful to me?

If I had one year left to live, what would I do?

What am I waiting for?

Do I know that if I am lucky enough to live until 100, almost every single person I love right now will be gone? How does that make me feel about living for the now? What do I feel I need to do differently with those I can still love right now, in this moment?

What limiting beliefs do I have that are impacting my ability to experience true happiness?

Gratitude

Use these pages to write or doodle all things that you are grateful for. Be as specific as possible and focus on the feelings that come up.

What kind of energy do I want to put into the world each day?

Do I believe in karma? If karma hit back, what would it be for? How would it affect my future?

How often do I listen to my intuition?

How do I know that I am listening to my inner tuition and not fears? What does it feel like?

What can I do to ensure I listen to my intuition and inner guidance more?

What's one problem I'm thankful I don't have?

If I were given a second chance, or a chance to redo something that has happened in my life, what would it be and why?

What life lesson did I learn the hard way?

What is the best advice I have ever been given? Why did I value it so much?

When was the last time I did something that I was afraid of? What was it and how did it make me feel?

Who is my biggest fan and why do they believe in me?

Why do I feel I was brought here to earth?

*If anything negative is written, go back and scratch it out.
Write the opposite positive.*

If I could offer advice to someone struggling with addictions or mental health challenges, what would it be?

How do I define addiction? Keeping in mind, addiction is not always drugs. It can be chasing happiness, lottery, food, pain, etc.

If you could bring one person back who has passed, who would it be and why? What would I want to talk about?

What areas of my life have room for growth?

How do I start nurturing those parts of me?

When things get tough, I would like to remember….

always remember these words

What is my truth when everything else is stripped away?

What is the meaning of life?

When was a situation that I was in the right place at the exact right time? How did it impact my life for the better?

What are 3 things I can do to improve my mental health?

1.

2.

3.

What would happen if I stopped worrying about what is bothering me?

If I were to ever be sent to jail, what would it be for and why?

If I could choose what I come back as in the afterlife, what would I be and why?

What are my top 5 bucket list items?

1.

2.

3.

4.

5.

If I could be a fly on the wall anywhere anytime (past, present or future), where would I choose and why?

What do boundaries mean to me?

What do I wish I could tell a specific someone, but am too afraid to?

Your secret is safe with this book, feel free to scratch out your answer after you write it

What is one small step I could take today to lead me closer to my goals?

Do I like who I have become? In what ways?

What is one part of my body that I am neglecting right now? What can I start doing to change that?

What is my definition of self care?

If I had a time capsule that would not be opened for 100 years, what would I put in it?

What would my superpower be if I could only choose one guaranteed to start today?

5 things I love most about myself and why.

1.

2.

3.

4.

5.

5 things that make me the happiest and why.

1.

2.

3.

4.

5.

Why am I enough, exactly as I am?

How can I express my love more into the world? How can I express more love for myself?

What is my favorite quote? Why?

How can I start to make someone's life easier? Who would it be and how?

If I could time travel to any year, what year would I pick and why?

If I could change one person, who would it be and why?

What mindset do I need to be in to feel in balance?

What's something I've always wanted to learn? What impact would it make on my life? How could I still learn it?

Gratitude

Use these pages to write or doodle all things that you are grateful for. Be as specific as possible and focus on the feelings that come up.

What is one belief I hold that some people may disagree with?

If I could only keep 3 things I have, what would they be and why?

1.

2.

3.

If I wanted to feel grateful right now, what could I think about?

What is one thing I am extremely passionate about? Why?

How can others benefit from my passion?

Here I am safe to write a letter to someone who has passed away…

Continue with Deep Breaths

What is the difference between living and just existing?

If I met a friend that I had not seen in 10 years, how would I tell him/her about my life right now?

What is something I have never told a single soul about before?

You can scratch this one out when you are done answering.

Is there a difference between happiness and fulfillment?

When is the last time I have asked people how my emotions have impacted them? If I ask, how do I think they will respond?

Bad Day Page

Here are some "bad day pages" to share your thoughts on the harder days when you have no where else to turn to.

Let it all out.

Be unfiltered, raw and real.

Use both sides of this page to scratch, scribble, rip the page out after - and breathe.

Bad days happen to all of us, but focus on the good days to come.

Rainbows follow after storms.

Bad Day Page

How can I begin to forgive myself?

What is one thing I know now that I wish I knew when I was younger?

Here I am safe to write a letter to someone who has hurt me, to forgive them and take the extra weight off my shoulders. I can thank them for the lesson, although painful, I grew into a better person.

What do I wish my parents/guardian did differently?

Do I understand that we are all born pure and perfect? Trauma and events happen over our lifetimes that change us. Do I agree with this statement? Why? Why not?

What do I have to do to see others as the pure form that we all originally started from? Will this be helpful or hurtful? Why?

What secrets am I holding onto and what harm are they causing?

What is the biggest battle I am facing right now? How can I help myself overcome it?

What is one past event that I previously perceived as a failure and now perceive as a gift?

What or who has been my greatest life teacher? What did I learn that means so much to me now?

What was the worst thing that has ever been said to me? How did it make me feel?

How have I healed from it? If I haven't just yet, what can I do to free myself from those words?

What does my inner critic tell me? Let us set it straight. Use powerful "I am" affirmations to correct your inner critic.

Scratch out all negative criticisms that comes up and replace them with positives.

Continue with Deep Breaths

What is something I have lied about before? Do I regret the situation?

Is there ever justification in lying? Why?

What do I keep saying yes to when I really mean no?

What do I want to be remembered for?

What am I holding on to that I need to let go of?

Write, draw or scribble all those words and feelings out on these pages. Give yourself time to get personal and deep dive. You are safe to let it go.

Continue with Deep Breaths

When I am 80 years old, what will matter to me the most?

If the average human lifespan was 50, what would I have done differently so far? (If older then 50, add 5 years to your age)

If I could give a newborn a piece of advice they would keep with them forever, what would it be and why?

Could I ever be like Nelson Mandela?

To elaborate, he was trialed and wrongfully sent to prison for 27 years. When he was released, he knew that if he stayed angry after leaving the jail he would never truly be out from behind bars. He chose to leave his anger and resentment behind him so he could be truly "free".

We all have the keys to our own jail cells, which doors do I need to close and finally free myself from?

Gratitude

Use these pages to write or doodle all things that you are grateful for. Be as specific as possible and focus on the feelings that come up.

What is one thing I have in common with someone who I have difficulties with?

Can I dig deeper and find something positive that I have in common with this person?

Here is a list of all the negative traits I have outgrown to be able to handle stressful situations with ease and grace.

What do I believe stands between myself and complete inner happiness?

How do I honour my truth?

Here is a list of the top 10 people I am thankful for in my life and one word to describe each person.

1.

2.

3.

4.

5.

6.

7.

8.

9.

10.

Who is one person, or stranger, that has a better life because I was a part of it, if even just for a moment? Who was it? What happened? How did the situation make me feel?

What loving advice could I give my enemy? If I do not have an enemy, someone I really don't see eye to eye with? Be gentle.

Here is a list of the people, or strangers, that have changed my life for the better. How did they help guide me?

What higher power do I believe in? Why?

When was a moment where I should have/could have died, but did not? What second chance was I given?

10 acts of kindness that I have done in my lifetime that I will never forget.

1.

2.

3.

4.

5.

6.

7.

8.

9.

10.

10 acts of kindness that others have done for me in my lifetime that I will never forget.

1.

2.

3.

4.

5.

6.

7.

8.

9.

10.

10 acts of kindness I would like to complete in the future

1.

2.

3.

4.

5.

6.

7.

8.

9.

10.

What are 3 moral rules I would never break?

1.

2.

3.

Why are the morals above so important to me?

The top 5 painful or happy experiences that have made me a better person today. How have I become a better person from these situations?

1.

2.

3.

4.

5.

Has my perspective changed at all while completing this journal?

What do I want to focus on for my outer world intentions once this journal is completed?

Why do I feel this book fell into my lap?

Digging deeper. Here I am safe to write a letter to my inner child. What would I want to say to them? What apologies would it include? I will be sure to soothe with my words, creating empowerment with teaching them about how far we have come. Empathy creates waves, I will make sure I speak in a gentle manner, reassuring my inner child and speaking from my heart. "I love you, I am sorry for the hurt you had felt, you don't need to hide anymore. I see you." I will thank my inner child for their bravery and their pureness. I will fill this letter with whatever I choose to, but I'll try to close the letter with positives.

To my inner child...

Continue on next page

Continue with Deep Breaths

What is my most beloved childhood memory?

If I had a chance to go back in time and change one thing, what would it be?

Paying attention to my feelings, what feelings came up as I wrote to my inner child? What were the positives and learning opportunities that flowed from those feelings? If I am still struggling with some of those feelings, the growth is still at my fingertips. I acknowledge how far I have come and remember that I was born pure. As we grow older, we experience traumas and sometimes that changes us, we can always circle back to the pure love that we were created to be.

The feelings I felt while writing my letter were...

Continue with Deep Breaths

Visualization Activity:

Sit quietly by yourself. Breathe deeply and relax, close your eyes, and start to visualize yourself walking down a flight of stairs to find a younger version of yourself sitting in front of you. Put yourself in a place, room, or memory that you are familiar with. Think deeply about the smells, feelings, who is surrounding you, the voices or sounds you hear, the way the room or area looks and sit down beside your child self. Smile, and start speaking to your child. Reassure them that they are: beautiful, powerful, kind, loving, pure, worthy of good things, smart, etc. Give your inner child any advice that comes to you – if you could share any words or advice with your inner child so pure and love filled – what would it be? Apologize to your inner child for any hurt they may have experienced. Close your visualization with a big bear hug together, smiling and wiping away any tears. Feel closure, warmth, and love towards the child as you come back into your now body.

Here I am safe to write a letter from my inner child to my adult self now. Tapping into the feelings of a child, in all pureness. What would my inner child have to say to the me that I am today?

My inner child would say...

Continue with Deep Breaths

Here I am safe to write a letter from the me now, to my future self.

Dear future me...

Continue with Deep Breaths

Gratitude

Use these pages to write or doodle all things that you are grateful for. Be as specific as possible and focus on the feelings that come up.

Can there be happiness without sadness? Peace without war? Pleasure without pain? Light without darkness? Why? Why not?

What harsh truths do I prefer to ignore?

Body, mind and soul check in. How am I feeling right now? How are my thoughts flowing? Negative or positive? If negative, what can I shift to change my perspective on some of the questions? Softening my shoulders, unclenching my jaw. Take a deep breath in, we got this.

What am I most afraid of?

What was my biggest childhood fear? How did I overcome it? If I haven't yet, how can I overcome it in the future?

Do I seek order or chaos? In what way?

What motivates me to get up every morning?

What gives me the most comfort?

What was my loneliest moment?

Bad Day Page

Here are some "bad day pages" to share your thoughts on the harder days when you have no where else to turn to.

Let it all out.

Be unfiltered, raw and real.

Use both sides of this page to scratch, scribble, rip the page out after - and breathe.

Bad days happen to all of us, but focus on the good days to come.

Rainbows follow after storms.

Bad Day Page

What was a character defining moment from my childhood?

If life was nothing but constant pain, would it still be worth living?

What is something I would like to say to my parents/guardians, but I could never tell them?

Am I choosing to break a cycle or pass the pain?

What's something I would do if I knew I could get away with it and no one would ever know?

What was the biggest adrenaline rush I've ever felt?

What is the most childish thing I still do?

What makes me feel unstoppable?

Has there been a time in my past where I wrongly 'judged a book by its cover?' What happened to change my view?

Gratitude

Use these pages to write or doodle all things that you are grateful for. Be as specific as possible and focus on the feelings that come up.

Is there such thing as "perfect"? Why or why not?

Is the glass half empty, or half full? What does your answer say about your perspective in life?

3x33 Rule
Write down an affirmation 33 times, 3 days in a row to focus my energy into the universe.

Day 1

1.

2.

3.

4.

5.

6.

7.

8.

9.

10.

11.

12.

13.

14.

15.

16.

17.

18.

19.

20.

21.

22.

23.

24.

25.

26.

27.

28.

29.

30.

31.

32.

33.

3x33 Rule
Write down an affirmation 33 times, 3 days in a row to focus my energy into the universe.

Day 2

1.

2.

3.

4.

5.

6.

7.

8.

9.

10.

11.

12.

13.

14.

15.

16.

17.

18.

19.

20.

21.

22.

23.

24.

25.

26.

27.

28.

29.

30.

31.

32.

33.

3x33 Rule
Write down an affirmation 33 times, 3 days in a row to focus my energy into the universe.

Day 3

1.

2.

3.

4.

5.

6.

7.

8.

9.

10.

11.

12.

13.

14.

15.

16.

17.

18.

19.

20.

21.

22.

23.

24.

25.

26.

27.

28.

29.

30.

31.

32.

33.

What are the 3 habits I would need to change to take my 'A' game to the next level? Why?

1.

2.

3.

Would I rather be rich or happy? Why?

What is my definition of rich?

55 people or things I have already manifested into existence

1.

2.

3.

4.

5.

6.

7.

8.

9.

10.

11.

12.

13.

14.

15.

16.

17.

18.

19.

20.

21.

22.

23.

24.

25.

26.

27.

28.

29.

30.

31.

32.

33.

34.

35.

36.

37.

38.

39.

40.

41.

42.

43.

44.

45.

46.

47.

48.

49.

50.

51.

52.

53.

54.

55.

What parts of life surprised me the most? What turned out the exact way I expected it would?

Do my goals truly reflect my desires?

What are 5 ways I can go out of my comfort zone this year by doing?

1.

2.

3.

4.

5.

If I could travel anywhere in the world, where would it be and why?

If I could have any job in the world, what would it be and why?

If I had 3 wishes, what would I wish for and why?

1.

2.

3.

I am safe to write down my dream life, without holding anything back – describing it in full details.

Continue with Deep Breaths

What is my ultimate goal in life?

What feelings would I feel if my goal came true?

Who would I share the good news with? What would that conversation sound like?

How would my dreams be the greatest good for all?

Dream Trip Manifestation Technique

Let's name the dream trip: _____
_____
_____

Where are you going? _____

Who will you bring with you? _____

What does it feel like to be there? _____
_____
_____
_____
_____
_____
_____

What smells do you favor there? _____
_____
_____

What do you see when you look out after you arrive? _____
_____
_____
_____
_____
_____
_____
_____

Now the finer details…

How long will you go for? _____

Where will you stay? _____
_____

What would you make sure you do when you're there?

_____
_____
_____
_____
_____
_____

How will you get there? _____
_____

Use Google or travelling apps to look up exact costs of what you would need to take your dream trip:

Flight: $ _____

Boat: $ _____

Train: $_____

Drive: $ _____

Hotel: $ _____

Hostel: $ _____

Personal Villa: $ _____

Other Expenses $ _____

Is it all inclusive, or would you bring/share meals with others?

_____
_____

What is the total cost to make it happen? $ _____

Be very detailed, try to think of every single expense to make sure you cover all bases.

Let the "how be the wow" because money comes to you in expected and unexpected ways, OR you can calculate it all, divide the cost over 5-10 years (however long you feel is fair) and either way it isn't just a dream – it's a reality YOU can make happen!

I will need to save $_____ per month to make my dream trip happen.

This challenge is to help visualize exactly what your dream trip consists of, and to show you that is isn't that far out of reach. Once you can see it in your mind, you can hold it in your hands.

Dream Life Manifestation Technique

Let's name your dream life: _____

_____

_____

_____

What does your dream life look like to you? _____

_____

_____

_____

_____

_____

_____

Is there a smell? _____

Is there a taste? _____

How does it make you feel to be in your dream life? _____

_____

_____

_____

_____

_____

_____

_____

What do you see? _____

_____

_____

_____

_____

What do you see surrounding you that is here in the physical still?

_____

_____

_____

_____

Get into the finest details possible. _____

_____

_____

_____

_____

_____

_____

_____

_____

_____

_____

_____

_____

_____

_____

Sit with what you write. Take the time to be specific and visualize yourself in this life. If you wish, you can create a vision board of photos and wording that describe your "dream life" and look at it every day.

This challenge is to help visualize exactly what your dream life consists of, and to show you that is isn't that far out of reach. Once you can see it in your mind, you can hold it in your hands.

What is one trait I picked up from my parents/guardian that I wish I didn't inherit? How do I change this trait?

Where do I want to be in the next 5 years?

What would I do with my life if money were not an issue?

If I lost my entire income source today, what would I start doing tomorrow to earn money fast?

What is something in my life that I would like to change, and what is stopping me from changing it?

What motivates me to keep going?

If I could share random advice with a stranger willing to listen at a bus stop, what would it be?

What would I regret if I died tomorrow?

What beliefs, fears and feelings can I remove that are holding me back from my deepest inner truth?

SCRATCH THEM OUT

SCRATCH THEM OUT

How do I measure success?

Can I only achieve what I set my mind to? Why or why not?

How am I feeling after completing this book? What have I learned about myself, my goals, my past and my feelings?

Extra spots for your thoughts...

Extra spots for your thoughts...